DATE DUE

MAY 0 5 2000	

DEMCO, INC. 38-2931

The Old Boy

THE
OLD BOY

A.R. Gurney

Garden City, N.Y.

To John Rubinstein and Paul Benedict,
who helped me immeasurably in trying to get it right.

THE OLD BOY was first produced at Playwrights Horizons (André Bishop, Artistic Director) in New York City, on May 6, 1991. It was directed by John Rubinstein; set design was by Nancy Winters; the costume design was by Jane Greenwood; the lighting design was by Nancy Schertler; the sound design was by Bruce Ellman and the production stage manager was Michael Pule. The cast was as follows:

DEXTER . . . . Richard Woods
BUD . . . . Clark Gregg
SAM . . . . Stephen Collins
HARRIET . . . . Nan Martin
PERRY . . . . Matt McGrath
ALISON . . . . Lizbeth MacKay

THE OLD BOY was revised and opened at the Old Globe Theater in San Diego, California, on January 18, 1992. It was directed by Paul Benedict; the set and lighting designs were by Kent Dorsey; the costume design was by Christine Dougherty; the sound design was by Jeff Ladman and the production stage manager was Peter Van Dyke. The cast was as follows:

DEXTER . . . . Franklin Cover
BUD . . . . Rob Neukirch
SAM . . . . John Getz
HARRIET . . . . Rosemary Murphy
PERRY . . . . Christopher Collet
ALISON . . . . Harriet Hall

CHARACTERS

SAM, middle-aged; Under Secretary of State for Political Affairs
BUD, younger; Sam's aide
DEXTER, older; Vice-Rector of a distinguished private boarding
   school
HARRIET, older; PERRY's mother
ALISON, middle-aged; HARRIET's daughter-in-law
PERRY, young; HARRIET's son

SETTING

The play takes place primarily at a distinguished Episcopal boarding
school in a small New England town during graduation weekend in
early June, now and in the past.

An open set, designed to accommodate a number of different playing
areas, indoors and out. Centrally located is the sitting area of the best
room in one of those old New England inns which service the private
schools near which they are located: a few pieces of good, simple
Early American furniture, particularly a bench, which will serve as a
couch, a student's bed, and ultimately the front seat of a car. Pictures
of the school, or of student teams, may be in evidence. There is also
an unobtrusive bar with liquor bottles, and a telephone somewhere
else. Scene shifts are indicated by changes in lighting and music.

The Old Boy

ACT ONE

In darkness: the sound of a boy's choir singing:

"Brightest and best of the sons of the morning, Dawn on our darkness, and lend us thine aid . . ."

The hymn fades into the sound of church bells chiming the hour —four p.m.—as DEXTER *enters the sitting area, followed by* BUD. DEXTER *is in his sixties, dressed in a seersucker suit, wearing a clerical collar.* BUD *is in his thirties, wears a summer suit and carries an attaché case.*

DEXTER (*proudly*): . . . And lo and behold! Our Celebrity Suite!

BUD (*looking around*): Uh huh.

DEXTER: We keep it specially reserved for guests of the school. There is a bar . . . two televisions . . . *three* telephones—including one in the bathroom, which always struck me as slightly excessive. . . . Do you think this will content your lord and master?

BUD: It's O.K.

DEXTER (*peering within*): Ah ha! I spy! His bags are already in the bedroom. I had them brought up during the press conference.

BUD: How come the press conference?

DEXTER: There seemed to be some demand.

BUD: I thought we agreed no publicity.

DEXTER: Oh well. Our school paper. . . . The local weeklies . . .

BUD: I thought we agreed.

DEXTER: Surely he can't steal in and out like a thief in the night.

BUD: I wrote you a letter. I spelled it out. This was to be a totally private visit. Then the minute we arrive, you set up mikes on the front lawn!

DEXTER: But he was proud and pleased. (*Going to a window*) Look at him, still surrounded by students. He's enjoying himself tremendously.

BUD: What about tomorrow?

DEXTER: Tomorrow?

BUD: When he makes the Commencement Address. Do you plan any PR?

DEXTER: I thought possibly our local station . . .

BUD: Radio?

DEXTER: Well actually it's a television station . . .

BUD: You're putting him on *TV?*

DEXTER: Oh just for local consumption . . .

BUD: The answer is No.

DEXTER: No?

BUD: No TV, under any circumstances.

DEXTER: May I take the liberty of asking why?

BUD: Because he's got a good chance to be nominated governor. We don't want to broadcast the fact that he's a closet preppy, sneaking on the old school tie.

DEXTER: Oh now really . . .

BUD: Private schools are political poison, Reverend. Take it from one who graduated from South Boston High.

DEXTER: Nonsense. Politicians are always trotting out Yale and Harvard.

BUD: Colleges are fine. You can earn your way there. But prep schools—forget it. They speak pull, they speak privilege. They go against the democratic grain.

DEXTER: Oh yes? Well I dare say that this school, because of its large endowment and generous scholarship program, is as democratic as any high school in the country. More so, in fact, because we draw students from all over the country— indeed, all over the world! It might be time for someone to stand up and publicly point that out.

BUD: Fine. But not him. And not tomorrow. And not on TV. Are we clear on that? (SAM *enters*)

SAM: What's the trouble? (SAM *is good-looking, well-groomed, middle-aged*)

DEXTER: I am being asked to hide your light under a bushel.

SAM: Bud is being political again?

BUD: Bud is being practical again.

SAM: Relax, Buddy. Loosen up. (*Looking around*) And hey! What a pleasant room.

DEXTER: Henry Kissinger spent a weekend here. And Helen Hayes.

SAM: Good Lord. Together?

DEXTER: Heavens no!

BUD: That's a preppy joke.

DEXTER: Oh. Ha ha. I see . . .

SAM: Actually, I think my father stayed in this room, the weekend I graduated.

DEXTER: He may well have. Wasn't he a trustee?

SAM: He sure was. And I remember, after the ceremony, he brought me back here, sat me down in this chair and offered me a dry martini. He said if I planned to drink, it was best I do it in front of him.

6

DEXTER: Ah yes. That was the standard approach to alcohol.

SAM: I'm glad it wasn't applied to fornication.

DEXTER: What?

BUD: Another joke.

DEXTER: Oh. Ha ha. Yes. I see.

SAM: Actually, the old man was a little late, as far as liquor was concerned. Little did he know that for three years, I'd already been sneaking out with the gang after the Saturday night movie, trying to get smashed on Wildroot Cream Oil Hair Tonic.

DEXTER: You, Sam? Winner of the Leadership Prize?

SAM: Oh, sometimes I led in the wrong direction.

DEXTER: I shouldn't know that. Now I'll have to suspend you immediately.

SAM: Good. That gets me out of my speech tomorrow.

DEXTER: You don't want to speak? To your old *alma mater?*

BUD: He jumped at the chance.

SAM: That's true. . . . But now I'm here, I feel as if I'm suddenly back on the debating team, knees shaking, stomach in knots, about to represent the school in a crucial contest against Andover. God, does anyone ever let go of this place?

DEXTER: Some of us feel it's important to hold onto.

SAM: Right. Of course. I'm sorry.

BUD: I need to phone. (DEXTER *indicates onstage phone*) I'll go in there. (*He goes off to the bedroom*)

SAM (*looking towards the bedroom*): What a big bed! A man could get lost in it.

DEXTER: How sad your lovely wife couldn't be here to share it with you. Wasn't her father in the class of '32?

SAM: That was my first wife.

DEXTER: Ah. Then I should have liked to meet her replacement.

SAM: She has her own agenda. You know wives these days.

DEXTER: Not well, I'm afraid.

SAM: You never married?

DEXTER: You might say I married the school. We've been together thirty-four years.

SAM: You've done better than I have . . . (*Looking toward the bedroom*) Now Bud there has a nice, stay-at-home wife, whom he's probably telephoning right now. And three sweet kids who call me "sir" when he brings them to the office.

DEXTER: Speaking of that, what do *we* call you, when we introduce you tomorrow? Mr. Ambassador? Mr. Congressman? What?

SAM: Oh I'll just settle for Your Majesty.

DEXTER: How about Mr. Governor?

SAM: That might be jumping the gun.

DEXTER: Oh now. Your young friend has high hopes.

SAM: We'll see . . . I suppose, when you have to be official, you could say Mr. Secretary. *Under* Secretary, way under, low man on the totem pole, but Secretary nonetheless. Otherwise I hope you'll just call me Sam. As you used to. When I was a boy here.

DEXTER: All right, Sam. And you should call me Dexter.

SAM: Not "Sir"? Not "Friar Tuck," which we called you behind your back?

DEXTER: Nowadays there's more alliteration involved.

SAM: I'll settle for Dexter.

DEXTER: Fine. And I'll ask the boys and girls to call you Mister.

SAM: Girls! I keep forgetting you have girls here now!

DEXTER: We have lots of things here now. We have a complete program in Asian studies. We have an active Hillel society.

And we have compulsory sex education for all entering students.

SAM: Compulsory sex? Sounds better than compulsory Latin.

DEXTER: No, I meant . . .

SAM: I know what you meant, Dexter, and I'm sorry. I apologize for all my asinine remarks. Ever since I came back, I've been systematically regressing into some adolescent wise guy. You should sting me with six demerits and confine me to study hall.

DEXTER: Now, now. Just as long as you give a good speech tomorrow.

SAM: Uh-oh. What if the trumpet giveth an uncertain sound?

DEXTER: Ah hah! You remember your Sacred Studies. "If the trumpet giveth an uncertain sound, who shall prepare himself for battle?" . . . Paul. First Corinthians.

SAM: Which I just read the other night.

DEXTER: Good heavens! Since when do politicians read the Epistles of Saint Paul?

SAM: When they're staying in some hotel. And can't sleep. And are tired of reading everything else. "Sounding brass and tinkling cymbal." That's me these days.

DEXTER: Oh now.

SAM: I'm serious. I guess that's really why I came back, Dexter. I have this uncontrollable need to return to the well.

DEXTER: I'm sure we can refresh you. Remember the words of our founding Rector: "No boy leaves this school unimproved." (BUD *comes out of the bedroom*)

BUD: I talked to the office. They say the Indonesian thing is heating up again. The White House wants you to call Jakarta and straighten things out.

SAM: Why do the Indonesians always wait till the weekend? (*He starts for the telephone*) If you'll excuse me, Dexter . . .

DEXTER: May I just raise one other small point, before you take up scepter and crown?

SAM (*stopping*): Shoot.

DEXTER: Do you remember a boy in your class named Perry Pell?

SAM: Of course! I was his Old Boy.

BUD: His what?

DEXTER: Old Boy. It's a system we have. A student who's been here—an Old Boy—or Old Girl, these days—is assigned to a New Boy, or New Girl, and guides him, or her, through the dark wood of the first year. Sam was an Old Boy to Perry Pell . . . (*Turning to* SAM) Who is dead, I'm afraid.

SAM: Dead?

DEXTER: He died last winter. Some accident, apparently.

SAM: I didn't know that.

DEXTER: Neither did the Alumni Office. His mother just told us.

SAM: I remember his mother.

DEXTER: And she remembers you. In fact, that's why she's here.

SAM: Here?

DEXTER: She heard you were delivering the Commencement Address, and up she came. I think she wants you to say a few words in memory of Perry.

SAM: Glad to.

DEXTER: I told her you had a very tight schedule, but perhaps she could stop by for a drink around five thirty, before we submit to the evening's festivities. I'll officiate, of course.

SAM: Fine with me.

DEXTER: Frankly, if I may speak briefly of treasures laid up on earth, she has proposed a major gift to the school in Perry's name.

SAM: Big bucks?

DEXTER: An indoor tennis facility. Two courts, a viewer's gallery, locker facilities—for both sexes, of course. She hopes you'll announce it tomorrow as well.

SAM: Of course. . . . Did Perry's wife come along, by any chance?

DEXTER: Actually, yes. You knew her?

SAM: She was my date for the senior dance. That's how he met her.

DEXTER: What a small world!

SAM: It was, then . . .

DEXTER: Well now I'll leave you to render unto Caesar the things that are Caesar's. (*He goes*)

SAM (*broodingly*): Perry Pell . . .

BUD: Sam.

SAM: Mmmm? Oh. All right. The Indonesian thing . . . (*Starts again for the phone*)

BUD: This stinks, Sam.

SAM: Now, now.

BUD: This sucks, man. I'm serious. I don't like this gig.

SAM: Something wrong with your room, Bud?

BUD: Sure. Per usual, they put me over the parking lot.

SAM: I'll tell them to change it.

BUD: They're using you, Sam.

SAM: Oh come on . . .

BUD: They're taking advantage! I make the deal, in and out, a quiet weekend in New England. And now suddenly you're giving cocktail parties, and announcing indoor tennis courts and doing preppy press conferences on the front lawn!

SAM: That's the first press conference I ever enjoyed.

BUD: And you got so chuckly and nostalgic I almost puked.

SAM: Easy, Bud.

BUD: Sam, we're running for the roses here! You have a clear track, all the way to November! There's only one little hitch in the whole picture, Sam.

SAM: And what is that, Bud, as if I didn't know.

BUD: The preppy thing.

SAM (*making it grimly portentous*): "The Preppy Thing."

BUD: No one likes Wasps any more, Sam.

SAM: The Irish adore us.

BUD: Not always, man. It's a love-hate thing.

SAM: You're Irish, Bud, and you love me.

BUD: I do love you—I mean, not *love* you, like you. . . . No, all right, love you. Don't tell Katie, but I do. I think you're the most decent guy I ever met. I'm betting on you, Sam. Which is why I quit my law firm, and took a salary cut of twenty grand, and am holed up here all weekend, overlooking a parking lot, rather than home with Katie and the kids. I mean, it bugs me, Sam! You were all signed up! Keynote speech at the National Conference of Mayors. Network coverage, hot issues, strong party support. Then Dexter calls, and you opt for this. People are pissed, Sam.

SAM: I know that.

BUD: Maybe you *don't* know how much I had to cover your ass, Sam. I piled story on top of story.

SAM: I appreciate it, Bud. Really.

BUD: Yeah, well, then what's the *real* story? Any thoughts? Now you're here?

SAM: I don't know. Maybe I'm like an Atlantic salmon. I got a whiff of those old headwaters, and just had to head upstream.

BUD: Don't salmon die when they do that?

SAM (*laughing*): *Pacific* salmon do, Bud. The Atlantic salmon tends to survive. . . . Oh hell, all I know is that there's something here. Something I missed, or lost, or need. Something I had to look for.

BUD: Then look for it *quietly,* O.K.?

SAM: Which means?

BUD: Which means don't stand up tomorrow, after you've reneged on a great speech on the problems of urban America, and in your best George Plimpton accent focus on a fancy tennis facility dedicated to some geek named Perry Pell. Please, Sam. That, don't do.

SAM: I—intend to pay my respects to a good friend.

BUD: Sometimes I think you don't want to win, Sam.

SAM: Sometimes I don't.

BUD: You'd better call the Indonesians.

SAM (*stretching out on the couch*): Suppose you take over the Pacific Rim this weekend.

BUD: What'll I say?

SAM: Say we deeply deplore whatever it is they're doing.

BUD: That won't wash.

SAM: Then tell them to do it our way.

BUD: They don't want to.

SAM: Then say the check is in the mail.

BUD (*taking his attaché case*): That'll fly. I'll be in my room. (*Starts out; stops; turns*) Don't get caught in this shit, Sam. Really. You've got too much to lose.

SAM: The past has a way of sneaking up on you, Bud.

BUD: So does the future . . . (*He goes off, as music comes up: a boys' choir singing: "Oh Paradise, Oh Paradise . . ."* SAM *gets up, takes off his jacket, looks out. Greenery and bird sounds*)

SAM (*now younger; calling out*): Come on, you guys! Many hands make light work! . . . Keep going! . . . Rake 'em into three main piles! (HARRIET PELL *appears in autumn light. She is a classy woman, with neat hair, wearing conventional, expensive clothes in the style of the early sixties. She calls to* SAM)

HARRIET: You there! Young man! May I speak to you, please?

SAM: Excuse me?

HARRIET: I'm looking for the young man in charge of the work program.

SAM: That's me.

HARRIET: Then you're our Old Boy! (*Calling off to* PERRY) I've found Sam, Perry! I've found our Old Boy! (*To* SAM) I'm already impressed. Making all those boys do all that work.

SAM: We all have to pitch in. It creates a sense of community.

HARRIET: Well I want to create a sense of Perry Pell. (*Calls off again*) Perry! We're waiting! (PERRY *comes on reluctantly; he is young, dressed in jacket and tie*) Perry, this is Sam. Shake hands, Perry. Good, firm grip. Look him right in the eye. (*The boys shake hands.* PERRY *moves away*) That's Perry, Sam. And I'm his mother. (*She holds out her hand*)

SAM (*shaking hands with her*): I figured.

HARRIET: I was very particular about selecting Perry's Old Boy. I asked for someone of the same age, in the same class, but who's been here a year. I want someone who plays sports WELL, and has recognizable leadership qualities. You obviously fill the bill.

SAM: Thanks.

HARRIET: I understand your father went here.

SAM: He's a trustee, actually. And my grandfather went here. And two uncles.

HARRIET: Mercy! You *are* an Old Boy! See, Perry? Sam knows the ropes, up and down the line. He'll help you fit in.

SAM: I'll sure try.

HARRIET: Now Sam, you should know that Perry is an only child.

PERRY (*quietly*): Mother . . . .

18

HARRIET: No, Darling. Sam should know that. He should also know that your father is totally out of the picture. (*To* SAM) I've had to take over from scratch in that department.

PERRY: Come on, Mother . . .

HARRIET: Sam should know these things, Dear. So he can whip you into shape.

PERRY: You forgot to tell him I'm toilet trained. (*He exits again*)

HARRIET (*laughing nervously*): He has an unusual sense of humor. (*Looks off*) But he retreats. He withdraws. He backs away. He goes to Washington with his school to visit the major monuments, ends up alone at the movies. He gets invited to his first formal dance last Christmas, winds up in a corner, reading a book. He reaches the semifinals of our local tennis tournament, and what? Defaults, so he can go to New York and visit his father.

SAM: Would he have won the tennis tournament?

HARRIET: No, Sam. No. I do not think he would have won. I think he would have lost. Because he refuses to go to the net.

SAM: No net game, huh?

HARRIET: No net game, Sam. Neither in tennis, nor in life. I'll bet you have a net game. (*They might sit together on the bench*)

SAM: Don't have much else.

HARRIET: Well Sam, you and I know, in our deep heart's core, that sooner or later people have to run to the net, and put the ball away. Otherwise, they lose. I hope your parents tell you the same thing.

SAM: My mother's given up tennis. She's not too well actually.

HARRIET: Oh dear. Nothing serious, I hope.

SAM: I hope . . .

HARRIET (*looks off*): Look at Perry, standing by that lake. Watch. Soon he'll start skipping stones. (*They watch*) See? That sort of thing can go on for hours! I'm all for marching to a different drummer, but this one won't march at all! (*Chapel chimes are heard. She gets up*) Well. I suppose it's time to go. (*Calls off*) I'm leaving, Darling! Time for the changing of the guard. (*To* SAM) Look how he walks. Just like his father. Who now slouches around Greenwich Village, calling himself an artist. (PERRY *comes on again*) Shoulders back, Darling. And goodbye. (*Kisses him*) Be strong, write lots of letters and pay attention to your Old Boy. (*Shakes hands with* SAM) Goodbye, Sam. I'm counting on you. (*She kisses* PERRY *again, and goes. Pause. The boys look at each other*)

SAM: Where's your stuff? (*No answer*) Where's your stuff, Perry?

PERRY (*very quietly*): Over at the dorm.

SAM: What?

PERRY (*louder*): Over at the dorm.

SAM: Met your roommate?

PERRY: Yeah.

SAM: Like him?

PERRY: He's O.K.

SAM: What about your bed?

PERRY: What about it?

SAM: Made your bed yet?

PERRY: No.

SAM: Come on. We'll go down to the dorm and make your bed.

PERRY: I don't want to make my bed.

SAM: You've got to make your bed, Perry. They have inspections. You get demerits.

PERRY (*almost inaudibly*): I don't think I'm right for this place.

SAM: Huh?

PERRY (*shouting*): I DON'T THINK I'M RIGHT FOR THIS PLACE!

SAM: Sssh. Hey. Go easy.

PERRY: I think I've made a serious mistake.

SAM: New boys always say that.

PERRY: No, it's not right for me. I can tell. Guys are playing hockey with Coke cans in the halls. I got stuck with the upper bunk. My roommate treats records like shit . . .

SAM: The first day always feels that way.

PERRY: No, I can tell when I'm not right for things. I wasn't right for boxing lessons. I wasn't right for Wilderness Camp.

SAM: I hear you're a great tennis player, though.

PERRY: I'm O.K. . . . Do guys ever run away from this place?

SAM: Not really.

PERRY: I might do it.

SAM: Run *away?*

PERRY: I might.

SAM: Where to?

PERRY: New York.

SAM: New YORK?

PERRY: Where my Dad lives.

SAM: You'd live with your Dad?

PERRY: I'll get my own place.

SAM: In New YORK? It's hugely expensive.

PERRY: I've got money. And I'll get a job.

SAM: Hey wow! You mean you'd just . . . (*Pause*) Well you can't.

PERRY: Why not?

SAM: You need an education, Perry.

PERRY: My grandfather quit school after seventh grade, and made sixty million dollars. Where do you get a taxi around here? (*Starts off*)

SAM: If you try to shove off, Perry, I'd have to turn you right in.

PERRY: Why?

SAM: Because . . . (*Pause*) Because I'm your Old Boy. I'm responsible for you.

PERRY: Just say you didn't know.

SAM: Nope. Can't. I promised your mother.

PERRY: Then I'll wait for another time.

SAM: Let's sit down for a minute. (*He indicates the bench*)

PERRY: I don't want to sit down.

SAM: Just sit. It doesn't hurt to sit—unless you have hemorrhoids. (PERRY *doesn't sit*) At least look out at the Lower School pond. (*More bird sounds*)

PERRY: I'm looking.

SAM: I noticed earlier you were skipping stones on that pond.

PERRY: And?

SAM: Didn't it kind of calm you down? Doing that?

PERRY: Maybe.

SAM: Know why?

PERRY: Why?

SAM: You were connecting with Nature.

PERRY: Get serious.

SAM: I *am* serious, Perry. Consider what you can do with that pond. You can skinny-dip in it, up by the dam. You can play hockey on it in the winter, you can build a raft on it in the spring. You can connect with it all during the school year. And whenever you do, you're connecting with Nature, Perry. And when you connect with Nature, it makes you a better guy.

PERRY: Save it for Sunday, O.K.?

SAM: No, it's true. I'm going to tell you something personal now. When I was a kid, I dreaded going here. I mean, my father entered me at BIRTH, for God's sake. I had no choice, even for another boarding school. My mom wanted me to stay at country day, but he vetoed the proposition. This was it. And when it came time to come, he just put me on the bus. My mom wasn't allowed to drive me up, because *his* mom didn't. "Throw him in the water, and he'll swim," my dad said. And the day I left, my mom and I were both crying, but he wouldn't even let us do *that*. I mean, your mom at least came WITH you.

PERRY: Don't remind me.

SAM: Anyway, here I was, stuck here, and at first I felt really low. So I took it out on people. I took it out on fat guys, for example. I'd tease them and grab their tits and all that. I mean, I was a real shit. But then I took a good long walk around the Lower School pond, and connected with nature, and now I honestly feel I'm a better guy.

PERRY: I don't mind fat guys.

SAM: Neither do I. Now. I *like* them, in fact. That's my point. And that's just an example of what happens here. What also happens is you get the finest education in the United States. You read Cicero in Latin in your Fourth Form year. You study European History, right on up to World War One. You read Shakespeare and Chaucer with the dirty parts left in.

PERRY: What dirty parts?

SAM: "The hand of time is on the prick of noon." How about that?

PERRY (*sarcastically*): Oh, I'm shocked! I'm disgusted!

SAM: O.K., so it doesn't hit you. So we'll shift to sports. Consider the athletic program.

PERRY: I read the catalogue, Sam.

SAM: All I'm saying, this is one great school. Guys all over the country are knocking themselves out to come here. The sons of two United States senators go here. The head of General Motors has his grandson right here. Katharine Hepburn's nephew goes here, and a kid whose mother was married to Ty Cobb. There are Jewish guys here now, and they raise the level of discourse, and Negroes on scholarship, who are a credit to their race. There are foreigners here, too—Japanese, and South Americans, and a kid from Hungary who took on Communist *tanks!* Oh, I'm telling you, Perry, if the Russians dropped a bomb on this place, it would cripple the entire free world!

PERRY: Aren't you slightly overdoing it?

SAM: O.K., but everyone here is a privileged person. And we have a responsibility to stay. We have a responsibility to take the courses, and go to chapel, and improve our bodies and our minds. That way, we become leading citizens. So if you ran away, you'd be turning your back on society and yourself.

PERRY: All you're saying is go make your bed. Right?

(*Pause*)

SAM: Right. (*He laughs*) I'm full of shit sometimes, aren't I?

PERRY: Yeah well who isn't?

SAM: No, but I sometimes get carried away. I'm glad you brought it to my attention, Perry. You'll be good for me. Just as I'll be good for you. Now. What about that bed?

PERRY: I guess I'll make it.

SAM: And I'll help you, Perry. And then we'll stir up a game of frisbee.

PERRY: I stink at frisbee.

SAM: We'll deal with that, Perry. We'll work on that. Meanwhile, do you know how to make hospital corners?

PERRY: No, frankly.

SAM: I'll show you how to make hospital corners. (*They run out. Another hymn: "Rise up, Oh Men of God . . ." DEXTER enters, carrying a tray of glasses, an ice bucket, and some potato chips*)

DEXTER: Room service, room service, courtesy of the school!

SAM'S VOICE (*from within*): Be right out!

DEXTER (*crossing to the bar*): No tipping, please! (*He sets the tray down, calls off the other way*) Ladies! I believe the gov-

A. R. Gurney

ernor is ready to convene the legislature. (HARRIET *and* ALISON *come in.* HARRIET *now looks older and wears contemporary clothes.* ALISON *is attractive and also well dressed*)

HARRIET (*looking around*): What a lovely room! Somewhat larger than those cubicles we've been assigned to! (SAM *enters, putting on his jacket and tie*)

SAM: Welcome, welcome.

HARRIET (*going to him*): Oh Sam! Dear boy! How good to see you again! (*She embraces him warmly*)

SAM: I'm so sorry about Perry, Mrs. Pell.

HARRIET: He adored you, Sam. He kept clippings from your whole career.

ALISON: Hello, Sam.

SAM: Alison. (*They kiss on the cheek*)

DEXTER (*officiating with the drinks*): Now who'll have what? Mrs. Pell?

HARRIET: Oh let's see. It's June, isn't it? I think I might be talked into a gin and tonic.

DEXTER: Gin and tonic it is.

HARRIET (*leading* SAM *to the bench*): Now sit here, Sam. Next to me.

DEXTER (*to* ALISON): Mrs. Pell, Junior?

ALISON: Just club soda, please. (*She sits off to one side*)

DEXTER: A little wine, for thy stomach's sake?

ALISON: No thank you. No.

DEXTER: Sam?

SAM: Light scotch, please, Dexter.

HARRIET: "Light scotch, please." I remember that very well. When you stopped by Grosse Pointe on your way west with Perry. Always light scotch.

SAM: Sometimes it wasn't so light.

HARRIET: Oh Sam, you've never gone overboard in your life.

ALISON: Oh yes he has. (SAM, HARRIET *and* DEXTER *look at her*) Long ago and far away.

HARRIET: Oh well, we all lose our grip occasionally. I did when I got married. But I came to my senses fast, let me tell you.

DEXTER: Sam, where's your ubiquitous amanuensis?

SAM: Who? Oh, you mean Bud.

DEXTER: Won't he join the dance?

SAM: Bud's in his room, proving that most of the important work in government is done by junior members of the staff.

ALISON: Isn't your wife here?

SAM: Couldn't make it.

HARRIET: Oh dear. And I hear she's perfectly lovely. She was a Thayer, wasn't she? From Philadelphia.

SAM: That was my first wife.

HARRIET: You traded her in?

SAM: Three years ago.

ALISON: The new one's name is Carol, and she has two children by her first marriage, just as you have two by yours, and you live in an old brick row house in Georgetown, where she runs a real estate office, and you serve the country at home and abroad.

SAM: Good for you.

ALISON: Oh I keep up.

SAM: You know more about me than I know about you.

ALISON: What's to know?

HARRIET: I'll tell you what's to know: Alison and Perry lived a lovely life together. They produced a sweet boy—my dear grandson . . . (*To* DEXTER) Who I hope will be admitted to this school the year after next.

ALISON: He's certainly been admitted to enough others.

HARRIET (*to* DEXTER): He has minor behavior problems.

ALISON: Which are threatening to become major.

HARRIET: He's in military school at the moment.

ALISON: Which he hates.

HARRIET: Which is ironing out a few wrinkles.

ALISON: If not burning a few holes.

DEXTER: I'm sure we can find a place for him, Mrs. Pell.

ALISON: If he wants to come.

HARRIET: How do they know what they want at that age? They must be pointed, they must be pushed.

ALISON: He might do better if he chose.

DEXTER (*passing a plate*): Potato chips, anyone? They're all I could drum up.

SAM: You look like you're serving Holy Communion, Dexter.

DEXTER: What? Oh dear. Ha ha. That's two demerits, for blasphemy.

HARRIET: Sam, I want to tell you about Perry. (*Pause*) It was a ghastly mistake. He misread his prescription, and took all the wrong pills.

ALISON: Oh . . .

HARRIET: Alison, of course, has a different opinion.

ALISON: The doctor has a different opinion.

HARRIET: Doctors don't know! I know Perry. I know that he'd never intentionally leave us without even saying goodbye. No. I'm sorry. No.

SAM: I'm sorry, too, Mrs. Pell.

HARRIET: I wish you'd been there, Sam. To keep him up to the mark.

SAM: We kind of lost touch after school.

HARRIET: He loved you, Sam. He loved this school. It was a turning point in his life.

DEXTER: That's why your gift will be so appropriate, Mrs. Pell.

HARRIET: He loved tennis, Sam.

ALISON: Well he didn't *love* it.

HARRIET: He won the Tennis Trophy!

ALISON: He liked other things more.

HARRIET: He won the Tennis Trophy here at school! He played on the Varsity at college!

ALISON: But he gave it up.

HARRIET: He loved the game, Alison. We watched Wimbledon together. Now stop contradicting.

ALISON: I wish . . . oh well.

SAM: What, Alison?

ALISON: I wish, instead of this tennis thing, it could be something to do with music.

HARRIET: As a me*mor*ial? For *Perry?*

ALISON: He loved music.

HARRIET: Couldn't play a note.

ALISON: He loved listening to it.

HARRIET: Music lessons for six years. Down the drain.

ALISON: But he listened to music all the time. What if there were some sort of place, with comfortable chairs, and good books all around, and a music collection, where people could put on earphones and listen to music, or read, or even sleep, if they wanted to.

HARRIET: That sounds very much like retreating to me.

ALISON: But Perry'd love a place like that.

HARRIET: That sounds like unconditional surrender.

ALISON: But—

HARRIET: I say tennis, Alison. And I happen to be paying the bill.

ALISON (*to* SAM): You can see how my mother-in-law and I get along.

HARRIET: Ah, but we always understand each other in the end, don't we, dear?

ALISON: I'm afraid we do.

HARRIET (*looking around*): I suppose you all think I'm a superficial woman simply interested in a snobby game.

DEXTER: Oh no. Heavens, no. Mercy, not at all.

HARRIET: Well, let me tell you something about tennis. When I was a girl, I was taught the game, and one of the things I learned was that every set, every game, every point is a new chance. As opposed to golf. There you are doomed from the start. Do badly on the first hole, you carry your mistakes on your back forever.

DEXTER: I see! What you're saying is that there is infinite salvation in tennis! Like Catholicism. Whereas golf is Protestant and predestined.

HARRIET: I don't know about that. I do know that when I was young, I made a mistake. I married the wrong man. But because I played *tennis,* I didn't feel I had to live with him for the rest of my life. I said, "All right, I've lost the first set. Time to change courts and start again." That's what I learned from tennis. And that's what Perry learned. And that's what I want the boys and girls at this school to learn, by playing tennis all year round. (*With a glance at* ALISON) Rather than slinking off into some corner to listen to what? *La Forza Del Destino?* Am I right or am I right, Sam?

SAM: Perhaps we shouldn't decide tonight.

ALISON: And the former Ambassador to Iceland once again exercises diplomatic immunity.

DEXTER: We DO have to decide whether or not to have our second drink here, or at Hargate, where the Rector and his Lady are waiting to greet us.

SAM: Let's go.

DEXTER: And then we'll proceed to the main dining room, where we will sup at the head table. Then, following our repast, and after the ladies have had a chance to powder their noses, we will attend the spring production of *All's Well That Ends Well.*

HARRIET (*taking* SAM's *arm as they go*): Poor Sam. You're stuck with us all evening.

SAM: All the more chance to hear about Perry.

DEXTER (*to* ALISON): After you, Mrs. Pell.

ALISON (*who has been staring off*): What? Who? Oh right, I keep forgetting that's me. Thank you. (*She goes out, followed by* DEXTER, *as the music comes up: the overture to* La Forza del Destino. PERRY *enters, in sweater and slacks, reciting, occasionally referring to a paperback playbook. He is very good*)

PERRY: "My father had a daughter lov'd a man
As it might be perhaps, were I woman,
I should your lordship. . . . She never told her love,
But let concealment like a worm i'th'bud
Feed on her damask cheek . . .
We men may say more, swear more; but indeed
Our shows are more than will; for still we prove
Much in our vows, but little in our love."

(SAM *enters, now wearing a sweater, hockey skates slung over his shoulder*)

SAM (*gesturing toward "the record player"*): Turn down the Farts of Destiny, will ya?

PERRY (*going to turn it off*): The Force of Destiny, Sam. *La Forza del Destino.* Jesus. You and that joke. We've heard it too many times.

SAM: We've heard the Farts of Destiny too many times. Bruiser MacLane says you're driving him batty with that record.

PERRY: He plays *Moon River* night and day.

Stephen Collins (left) as Sam with Nan Martin as Harriet

All photos of the 1991 off-Broadway production at the Playwrights Horizons Studio Theatre by Joan Marcus.

Matt McGrath as Perry

Nan Martin as Harriet

Stephen Collins as Sam

SAM: That's different. Yours is an opera.

PERRY: What's wrong with opera?

SAM: Bruiser says it's fifty percent fag.

PERRY: Oh come on . . .

SAM: He *knows*, Perry. He's from San Francisco!

PERRY: Stop playing Old Boy, Sam. That was last year, O.K.?
(SAM *throws himself on the "bed"*)

SAM: O.K. Fine. Play what you want. Who gives a shit?

PERRY: What's eating you?

SAM: Nothing. (*Pause*) Except I just got a call from the old man.

PERRY: And?

SAM: He can't take me skiing at Stowe spring vacation.

PERRY: Why not?

SAM: Too expensive. He SAYS. But I think he's got a girl.

PERRY: Well that happens. I mean, your mom's been gone almost a year.

SAM: I know it happens, Perry. I'm not dumb. (*Pause*) I also know he doesn't love me.

PERRY: Oh come on . . .

SAM: He *likes* me. But he doesn't love me. I used to think if I did well, if I won prizes and stuff, maybe he'd love me. But now I wonder.

PERRY: At least he leaves you alone.

SAM: Look, your mother wants the best for you because she thinks you deserve it. My dad thinks I'll never really measure up. That's the difference. (*Pause*) Anyway. Spring vacation. Maybe I'll come south and hook up with you.

PERRY: Actually, I'll be in New York spring vacation.

SAM: I thought the tennis team planned to practice in South Carolina.

PERRY: I'm not playing tennis this year.

SAM: WHAT?

PERRY: I decided to be in the spring show.

SAM: Do both, for God's sake.

PERRY: Can't. I got a lead role, and the tennis team has too many games away.

SAM: But you're due to play second on the varsity this year!

PERRY: That's the way the ball bounces.

SAM: All I can say is it better be one hell of a good play.

PERRY: It's Shakespeare.

SAM: Oh God, not again. What play?

PERRY: *Twelfth Night,* actually.

SAM: That's not such a great play, Perry. I got a C minus on that one.

PERRY: I like it. A lot.

SAM: You playing that duke?

PERRY: No actually, not.

SAM: Then who? One of those clowns who think they're so funny?

PERRY: Actually, I'm playing Viola.

SAM: Viola? You mean the *girl?*

PERRY: She's a boy all during the play.

SAM: But she's really a girl.

PERRY: She wears pants all the way through.

SAM: But she is definitely a *girl,* Perry.

PERRY: O.K. she's a girl.

SAM: You played a girl last year.

PERRY: I played Mercutio last year.

SAM: You also played a girl.

PERRY: In the musical. Because they asked me too. I won the prize for Mercutio.

SAM: Perry, let me say something here. Now how do I put this? You and I are good friends now, right?

PERRY: Right.

SAM: I mean, we're way beyond last year's Old Boy shit. I mean, when my mother died, and I wanted to bug out, *you* were the Old Boy, actually. You got me to stay.

PERRY: Misery loves company.

SAM: Yeah, well we're even. This is just friends talking. Friend to friend. And I'm not saying this just for an excuse to go south spring vacation, either. What I'm saying is I really don't think you should take that part in that play, Perry.

PERRY: Here beginneth today's bullshit.

SAM: No, but remember last year? That Fairy Perry stuff?

PERRY: That's over now.

SAM: Because of your *tennis* it's over! I'm telling you, you play another girl, and keep up this opera crap, it'll start up again! It's a bird, it's a plane, it's Fairy Perry!

PERRY: Knock it off, O.K.

SAM: They even called *me* a fairy for hanging out with you. That's how I got in that fight that time. I was defending *both* of us.

PERRY: I can defend myself, Sam.

SAM: You'll have to, if you take that part.

PERRY: Fat Pig Hathaway gets those pig jokes all the time. Piggy-piggy. Soo-ey. Oink oink. He lives through it.

SAM: What you don't know is, Perry, Fat Pig had to see a psychiatrist last summer. He had to cancel a canoe trip.

PERRY: Alas and alack.

SAM: I'm *serious*, for Chrissake. The choices you make in school are extremely significant, Perry. They can have an important effect on your later life.

PERRY: O.K. Now apply the bullshit quotient: divide that by two point five . . .

SAM: Oh hell. I give up. (*Pause*)

PERRY: In Shakespeare's time, boys played all the girls' parts.

SAM: I know that.

PERRY: Same with the Greeks. Same on up to the seventeenth century. Guys played girls all the time.

SAM: Who doesn't know that?

PERRY: Yeah well, no one ran around calling them fairies, Sam. They were considered first-rate guys. Actors from Athens served as ambassadors to Sparta.

SAM: No wonder Athens lost the war.

PERRY: Ha ha. Big joke. Remind me to laugh some time.

SAM: I just can't believe you like acting better than tennis.

PERRY: I like—being someone else.

SAM: It's kind of weird, when you think about it, Perry.

PERRY: Maybe I'm weird then.

SAM: Well people who are weird work on the problem. They try *NOT* to be weird.

PERRY: Maybe I like being weird. Ever think of that?

SAM: Didn't you like it when you beat that guy from Exeter in the JV match last year? Three great sets, the last one ten–eight. Didn't you like that?

PERRY: I loved that!

SAM: Yeah, but it's not weird enough, huh. So you're going to give up a major slot on the Varsity Tennis Team, which could make you captain next year. Which could get you into Columbia, which is in New York City, your favorite place. Which won't happen if your grades go down because you spend too much time rehearsing plays, playing a girl. (*Pause.* SAM *looks at his watch*) Well, I'm late for the debating society. Maybe I'll do better over there. (*Starts out*)

PERRY: Sam. (SAM *stops*) You did O.K.

SAM (*coming back in*): If you played tennis, we could end up in Florida. We could check out the Yanks in spring training! Your favorite team, man!

PERRY: Get going, Sam. (SAM *starts out again, then stops again*)

SAM: I just wish you'd talk to Bruiser MacLane, that's all. He'll tell you about *real* fairies. Guys who look at you in the men's room. Guys who—

PERRY: Get out of here, Sam!

SAM: O.K., but think tennis, man! (SAM *runs off, as* PERRY *stands looking after him. He gets his Shakespeare book, ponders it, then goes slowly off, as a hymn comes up: "Creations, Lord . . ." It becomes dark on stage.* BUD, *in his shirt sleeves, comes in, holding a FAX sheet*)

BUD (*toward bedroom*): Sam? (*He turns on a light, goes to the telephone, dials quickly*) Hi. It's me. . . . Give me Bill again. . . . Bill, I just picked up your FAX down at the desk. Now listen: you checked this out, right? I don't want to go out on a limb here, man. . . . You're sure then? (SAM *comes in from the hall*) Uh huh . . . uh huh . . . Thanks. I'll return the favor, Bill. (*Hangs up*)

SAM: Still burning the midnight oil, Bud? I thought we were all to make a conscious effort to conserve energy.

BUD: How was *All's Well That Ends Well?*

SAM: Fine, except for the ending.

BUD: This FAX just came in from Washington.

SAM: About Indonesia?

BUD: About your friend. . . . How he died.

SAM (*taking it*): Thinking of transferring to the F.B.I., Bud?

BUD: You asked.

SAM: I didn't ask *you.*

BUD: I happened to have a call in to Treasury. The guy on night security ran a quick check.

SAM: I know how he died, Bud.

BUD: I don't think you do.

SAM (*reads, looks up*): AIDS?

BUD: Suicide. Because of AIDS. Made it look like an accident. To make it easy on his family.

SAM: You sure?

BUD: I double checked. (*Pause*)

SAM: Go to bed, Bud.

BUD: Still plan to make a speech about this guy?

SAM: Of course.

BUD: You still plan to make a speech, at a posh prep school, with the primary right down the road, at a time when people who are HIV positive can no longer get into the *country,* about a close friend who died of AIDS?

SAM: I said I would.

BUD: If our friends on the Right get wind of this . . .

SAM: I'll deal with that.

BUD: Let me write it, then.

SAM: You didn't know him.

BUD: All the better.

SAM: Bud . . .

BUD: This is a minefield, Sam. (*Knocking from off*) Christ. Who's that? Jesse Helms?

SAM (*calling*): Come in. (ALISON *comes in*)

ALISON: Am I interrupting something?

BUD: Looks like I am.

SAM: Bud's going to bed.

BUD: Bud's going to work. (*He leaves*)

ALISON: I'm sure he thought I was here to seduce you.

SAM: Why would he think that?

ALISON: Because that's what I plan to do.

SAM: Damn! I planned to seduce *you*.

ALISON: We can take turns.

SAM: I take it you got my little note.

ALISON: Found it under my door.

SAM: I figured the bar downstairs was about to close, and since I have this sitting room . . .

ALISON: Absolutely. And I got Harriet to go straight to bed. I heard her snoring like a soldier when I tiptoed past her door.

46

SAM: May she dream of Swedish tennis stars, all running to the net.

ALISON: Amen.

SAM: So. Here we are.

ALISON: The Old Boy and his Old Girl. `. . . Do you ever think about those days?

SAM: I'm thinking about them now.

ALISON: That summer on Martha's Vineyard . . .

SAM: Ah. The Vineyard . . .

ALISON: No cracks, please. It was home to me. My father ran the hardware store, remember?

SAM: What I remember is the sail locker of the Edgartown Yacht Club.

ALISON: Don't rush things.

SAM: You're right. If I'm going to re-seduce you, I should ply you with alcohol.

ALISON: The way you did then? With scotch? Stolen from the Yacht Club bar?

SAM: What'll you have this time?

ALISON: Nothing, thanks.

A. R. Gurney

SAM: Given it up?

ALISON: Trying to.

SAM: You and everyone else in the post-Industrial World. Makes it tougher to seduce people. (*Makes himself a drink*) You look terrific, by the way.

ALISON: Do I look to the manner born?

SAM: You sure do.

ALISON: Good. I've been working on it since the day we met.

SAM: Do you remember that day?

ALISON: Totally. I was waitressing at the Clamshell, earning money for college.

SAM: And I was visiting Kip Farraday, from school.

ALISON: Whoever. I never knew your names. All I knew was you moved in a flock. The annual migration, the June arrival of the summer boys, with your white teeth, and old sneakers, and no socks, and great wads of money stuffed in your Bermuda shorts.

SAM: Not much in mine.

ALISON: No. You were different. The flock blew into the Clamshell, and blew out, but you stayed. And ordered another cheeseburger. And introduced yourself.

SAM: And asked you to the movies . . .

ALISON: And to the beach the next day. But I'll have you know it took you a week to get me into that sail locker.

SAM: Do you remember I rigged up a bed for us with someone's silk spinnaker?

ALISON: I remember everything. That was my first time.

SAM: Mine, too.

ALISON: I know. (*Pause*) It was a lot of firsts. It was the first time I began to wonder where you came from, you summer boys. Suddenly all I wanted in the world was to get off that island, and see where you went after Labor Day.

SAM: And so you did.

ALISON: Yes I did. Thanks to you. What a gentleman you were! Inviting me up here for that dance. That was another thing summer boys didn't do.

SAM: I hope you had a good time.

ALISON: Oh I did! (*Pause*) No, I didn't. (*Pause*) My shoes were wrong. (*Pause. She looks at her feet*) Well, they're right now, goddammit.

SAM (*getting close to her*): I like the shoes.

ALISON: Thank you.

SAM (*nuzzling her*): I like what's in them.

ALISON: Still the same old line, I see.

SAM: Sure you won't have a drink?

ALISON: No thanks. I'm not an alcoholic, I don't think, but liquor gets me going.

SAM: All the more reason.

ALISON: I think we should talk about Perry.

SAM: I know about Perry.

ALISON: The whole story?

SAM: Enough. Bud did some homework. Are you all right?

ALISON: Me? Oh you mean, my health? Sure. Fine. I had myself thoroughly tested. It was unlikely, anyway. We hadn't slept together for years. So you see it's perfectly safe for you to be seduced.

SAM: Poor Alison.

ALISON: No, actually, *not* poor Alison. Rich Alison, which was what I wanted. They say if you marry money, you end up earning every cent of it.

SAM: Was it grim?

ALISON: Not for a while. We had one hell of a good time at first. Perry was lavishly affectionate. And we had great fun. We bought this gorgeous house outside of town, had horses, dogs, even a baby. Money does a lot, Sam. It kept us going for quite a while. Until he announced he was gay.

SAM: Announced?

ALISON: Sat me down one day, and told me point blank. And I said, "Oh, don't be silly, just because our sex life is a little dicey lately," so then he said he'd just made love with the man who cleaned the pool. I remember hearing that goddam *Forza Del Destino* blaring away in the background.

SAM: Oh boy.

ALISON: So I said get out. Darken our pool-house no more. Something like that. (*Pause*) Do you think I would have said that if it had been a woman? (*Pause*) I know he never said it when I'd been with men. (*Pause*) Maybe I will have a drink after all.

SAM: You're sure, now? (*Chapel chimes are heard*)

ALISON: I am sure. How about rye and ginger, for old times' sake?

SAM: There's neither one.

ALISON: Then vodka. Straight. Thanks. (SAM *pours it*) Aaanyway, off he went, into outer darkness. And then came the explosion. He must have been building up steam all along. Lover after lover after. . . . But did I get divorced? Not this

51

cookie! Oh no. I bided my time. Why? Money. Harriet paid the hush money, or whatever you want to call it. And I was free to continue a few discreet relationships of my own. Then, when he got sick, I couldn't . . . I mean, I couldn't just . . . I mean, he was *dying*.

SAM: Were you . . . hey, do you mind these questions?

ALISON: I like them. You're the first person who's had the guts to ask.

SAM: Were you with him when he died?

ALISON: No. By then, he had found his one true love. In his precious New York. A dear man who runs a travel agency. And who took care of him. And helped with the pills. And came to the funeral. And cried. Well, we all cried.

SAM: Poor guy. Not even saying goodbye . . .

ALISON: I know. That sweet man. We loved each other, in a way. In a good way. Of course, it wasn't . . . the way he felt about his final friend. Or the way I felt about you.

SAM: Uh oh.

ALISON: Oh no. Don't worry. We played that scene out years ago. Remember? The old Whaler Bar, on Madison Avenue, the day after Labor Day? Me tossing down rye and gingers and spilling my guts all over the table. You sipping your goddam scotch. And spurning me.

SAM: I didn't "spurn" you, Alison.

ALISON: You said you didn't love me.

SAM: I said I didn't love you enough.

ALISON: Enough for what, for God's sake?

SAM: Enough to stay faithful, at different colleges, all the next year. Enough to get married after we graduated. Which is what you wanted.

ALISON: Your father didn't like me.

SAM: He didn't know you.

ALISON: He didn't want to know me.

SAM: He didn't think I was ready to get involved.

ALISON: But Perry was.

SAM: Seems so.

ALISON: You told me he was.

SAM: Did I?

ALISON: But you didn't tell me Perry was gay.

SAM: I didn't know Perry was gay.

ALISON: Oh Sam.

SAM: I didn't believe it.

ALISON: Oh Sam.

SAM: I thought he could change.

ALISON: You thought I could change him.

SAM: Maybe.

ALISON: The Old Boy passes the ball to the Old Girl.

SAM: Oh come on.

ALISON: Yes, well, I tried. I tried very hard.

SAM: Oh Alison.

ALISON: And if I ultimately didn't succeed, at least I ended up in that golden land where the summer boys came from.

SAM: Otherwise known as Grosse Point.

ALISON: Exactly. Sometimes it's very gross, and sometimes there's no point, but I got what I wanted in the end. (SAM *goes for another drink;* ALISON *holds out her glass*) Where are your manners?

SAM: Already?

ALISON: Why not? (SAM *makes her another*) Gosh. I suppose this is what makes you such a good politician. You have a drink with people, and before long they're spilling the beans, and you've got them in your pocket.

image_001.png

SAM (*bringing her drink*): Pocket, hell. I'm trying to get you in my bed. (*He touches her hair*)

ALISON: Hey! No fair! I've stripped down, I'm sitting here stark naked, and you're still buttoned to the nines! (*She kicks off her shoes*)

SAM: What do you want to know?

ALISON: I'm not even sure. I've read so much about you. You were even in the magazine on the airplane, coming east. Harriet pointed it out to everyone in First Class.

SAM: Oh well, it's been mostly luck and pull.

ALISON: Don't be modest.

SAM: I'm serious. Mostly appointments, mostly through the Old Boy network. Kip Farraday, the guy from the Vineyard, got me my first job in the State Department, and I've been shunting around ever since.

ALISON: Aren't you running for governor in the fall?

SAM: If I'm nominated.

ALISON: Big step.

SAM: So they tell me. I'm trying to get cranked up for it.

ALISON: You don't want it?

SAM: I *want* to want it. That's about as far as it goes. Frankly, Alison, I have to say . . . I've been feeling a little . . . bankrupt lately. About what I do. I mean, I'm still writing the checks, but I'm not sure the money is there any more.

ALISON: Sounds like you'll make a good governor.

SAM (*laughing*): Thanks. (*They kiss*)

ALISON (*finally breaking it off*): Hey! What about the lovely second wife, who sells condos in Washington and looked so trendy in *Vanity Fair?*

SAM: Ah. (*Pause*) We're getting divorced. She's shoving off as soon as the political dust settles.

ALISON: Well, well.

SAM: It's tough being a politician's wife. I'm not always there, and when I am . . .

ALISON: You're not always there.

SAM: Exactly.

ALISON: Some rag I read in the supermarket called you a womanizer.

SAM: Whatever that means . . .

ALISON: It means you run around screwing women.

SAM: Hmmm.

ALISON: Do you?

SAM: Yes. Sometimes. Yes. Recently, too much so.

ALISON: Why?

SAM: Wish I knew.

ALISON: Sounds like you're going through your own explosion.

SAM: Maybe so.

ALISON: You and Perry. And me. All trying to make up for lost time. (*Pause*)

SAM: Let's make up for it right now. Come on. I'll rig the bedroom up like a sail locker.

ALISON: I think we're beyond the sail locker now.

SAM: I suppose we are.

ALISON: I think we've arrived at the Biltmore Hotel. Remember the Biltmore? The plan was to spend a fantastic night there before we went off to our colleges.

SAM: O.K. Let's pick up where we left off.

ALISON: God, you were the perfect gentleman. You took my arm and walked me there, after our big scene at the Whaler Bar. You checked me in. You stayed with me while I simmered down. You even lent me your handkerchief, which I still have. But like many gentlemen, you neglected to pay the bill.

SAM: Your bill was paid, Alison.

ALISON: Not by you, it wasn't.

SAM: Perry paid the bill.

ALISON: How do you know that?

SAM: And drove you up to college afterwards.

ALISON: How do you know that, Sam?

SAM: I asked him to.

ALISON: You ASKED him to?

SAM: I suggested it.

ALISON: I never knew that before.

SAM: You think I'd leave you stranded in some strange hotel?

ALISON: I always thought it was just luck, coming down in the morning, seeing Perry waiting in the lobby, under the clock. He never told me it was prearranged.

SAM: Because he was a gentleman, too.

ALISON: Of course! Dumb! Dumb me! I should have known! Both of you, gentlemen, all the way. You didn't want to dance with me any more, so you got your friend to cut in.

SAM: I thought I was doing the right thing.

ALISON: Fuck the right thing!

SAM: Hey! Go easy.

ALISON: I'm suddenly feeling a little set up, Sam!

SAM: I think that is rather a bald way of . . .

ALISON: I'm beginning to feel you set up my whole damn LIFE!

SAM: Oh now hey, Alison.

ALISON: And never a call, to either of us, after you did it. Just a wedding present, card enclosed.

SAM: I thought it best not to interfere.

ALISON: Oh sure. The Under Secretary of State sets up a puppet regime and then walks away from it. (*She goes to the bar*)

SAM: Maybe you've had enough.

ALISON: Maybe I haven't. . . . Do you still think it was the Right Thing, knowing what you know now?

SAM: I think . . . I think we should terminate this little brush-up course in ancient history. We're not getting anywhere.

ALISON: I'm getting somewhere.

SAM: Oh yes?

ALISON: You know why I came up here this weekend? I wanted to show you how well I've survived after all these years.

SAM: As indeed you have . . .

ALISON: I also wanted to go to bed with you and show you that little old Alison Shaeffer from the Clamshell still knows how to do it!

SAM: You might keep your voice down.

ALISON: But now I know I don't want that at all. All I want to hear is you say something along the lines of "I'm sorry."

SAM: I'm perfectly willing to say . . .

ALISON: No! You'll never say it! Not really! Not you! Not you and all the other old, old BOYS in your fucking CLUB, moving your same dead old ideas around the backgammon board down in Washington!

SAM: I think you may have had too much to . . .

ALISON: Moving PEOPLE around, too! Moving kids off to Viet Nam and the Middle East and Lord knows where it'll be next! Moving ME around, goddammit! Moving Perry! Oh Christ, I thought I came to show you my shoes, but now I'd like to use them to brain you, you goddamn son of a bitch! (*She throws a shoe at him*)

SAM (*backing off*): Hey, come on, please . . .

ALISON: Oh hell. Don't worry. That wouldn't do any good, either. I'd never be able to bash my way through that thick shell you guys have built around yourselves all these years, no, wrong, all these GENERATIONS! (*She finds her shoe, puts it back on*) No wonder your wives give up, trying to break in! No wonder you fool around, trying to break out! Well let me tell you something, Mr. Old Boy! *I'm* sorry! ME! I'm saying it to you. Know why? Because I don't think you've ever loved anyone. Love? You don't know the meaning of the word! You wouldn't know it if it stared you in the face! (*She storms out.* SAM *stands, staring after her. A hymn comes up: "Ten Thousand Times, Ten Thousand. . . ." Fade to black*)

END OF ACT ONE

ACT TWO

ACT TWO

The ringing of church bells. SAM, *looking disheveled, with rumpled hair, in his shirt sleeves, sits writing on a note-pad, sipping coffee. After a moment, the sound of knocking.*

SAM (*calling out*): It's open! (BUD *comes in, dressed as before. He carries his briefcase*)

BUD: You look awful.

SAM: Thanks.

BUD: No, you do.

SAM: I didn't get much sleep last night.

BUD: Who does around here? Christ, between drunken parents arguing in the parking lot, and those fucking bells! . . . Goddammit, ding-dong!

SAM: The Call to Worship, Bud. In about a half an hour, we're going to stride manfully to the Chapel, where for a rather long hour, we will thank thee, Lord, Our God, with hearts, and hands, and voices. (*He returns to his work*)

BUD (*glancing toward the bedroom*): All clear, by the way?

SAM: Of course it's all clear.

BUD: She left?

SAM: She didn't stay.

BUD: That's something new.

A. R. *Gurney*

SAM: No comment. (*Again he returns to his work*)

BUD: You really do look kind of beat, Sam.

SAM: I'll get fixed up.

BUD: I brought along some of that pancake they gave you on MacNeil-Lehrer. Want me to get it?

SAM: Nope. (*He crumples up a paper*)

BUD: What the hell are you doing?

SAM: Trying to figure out what to *say.*

BUD (*opens his folder*): I've said it. Right here. I'm quite proud of it, actually. After some passionate remarks about the need for new standards in American education, I modulate neatly into a discussion of public health, and wind up with a tender plea for human compassion.

SAM: You're a cynical bastard, Bud.

BUD: I like to win, Sam.

SAM: Think I'll do this one on my own, actually.

BUD: Yes? It doesn't look like you're getting very far.

SAM: I haven't, yet.

BUD: You've got twenty minutes before the schedule kicks in. (*Reading from his folder*) Services in the chapel at ten. Cof-

66

fee for special guests in the vestry at eleven-fifteen. Commencement exercises begin promptly at noon.

SAM: Then I'll wing it.

BUD: *Wing* it? *You?*

SAM: I've done it before.

BUD: Oh sure. With the League of Women Voters?

SAM: That was O.K. (*He starts off to get dressed*)

BUD (*calling after him*): What? The Q. and A. was a ritual castration.

SAM: What about the Gridiron Club?

BUD: Oh right. When you tried to be funny.

SAM: I was funny. I got a huge laugh.

BUD: That was a groan, Sam. A universal groan.

SAM: Anyway, this will be different. I know my audience better.

BUD: That's what scares me. You'll get all preppy and in-group, the way you were at that press conference.

SAM (*as he gets dressed*): You think so, Bud? Why? All I plan to do is open with a couple of sly, demeaning jokes about blacks and women. Then, after some comments about trust funds and deb parties, I'll slip into the main body of my speech, pleading passionately for lower capital gains taxes and higher caliber handguns. I'll try to season these thoughts, of course, with vigorous, contemporary language: "Gosh," I'll say, and "What the Dickens!" and even "Darn it all!" Toward the end, I'll toss in a few subtle anti-Semitisms, but gee whiz, Bud, most of those will be directed strictly against Israel. Finally, I'll refer to my old friend Perry, but I'll be so tight-assed and tongue-tied that it will only show that I'm totally out of touch with my own feelings.

BUD: You're kind of hyper today, aren't you?

SAM: Oh yes I am, Bud. Yes I am. So hyper that when the ceremony is over, I plan to dash back here and change into my pink polo shirt and lime-green pants with little whales on them. Then, after too many martinis, and too few chicken sandwiches—on white bread—with the crusts cut off—I'll just drive recklessly off into the sunset in my green Volvo station wagon for an adulterous affair with the waitress at the local cocktail bar.

BUD: That last little detail has the ring of truth.

SAM: Oh hell, Bud. Lighten up.

BUD: I'm thinking of your career, Sam.

SAM: And your own.

BUD: Sure, my own. Katie called last night.

SAM: What else is new?

BUD: I'll tell you what's new. What's new is a new offer from my old law firm. Six figures. With a guaranteed partnership in three years. That's what's new.

SAM: What does Katie think?

BUD: She wants me home. The kids want me home. The dog wants me home.

SAM: What about the cat?

BUD: The cat can't make up its mind. . . . And neither can I, Sam. I said I'd decide today.

SAM: You mean you'd quit on me? Even before the convention?

BUD: I want to stay, Sam. Really! I want to go all the way to the top right by your side. There are some guys, they walk into a room, and you like them, you trust them, you could work for them easily all the days of your life! You're one of those guys, Sam. I sensed it when I met you, and the voters will sense it, too. You're our best shot in this weird world, and if you'll just keep your eye on the goddamm ball, you could be president one of these days!

SAM: And you think I'd mess that up if I said a few words about a dear, dead friend.

BUD: I think you might. Yes.

SAM: Well I'm sorry. I have certain loyalties . . .

BUD: Maybe it's time to stop playing Old Boy, Sam.

SAM: Maybe you're getting a little big for your britches, Bud.

BUD: Which is an Old Boy expression if I ever heard one.

SAM: Bug off, Bud.

BUD: Fuck you, Sam!

SAM: Watch the language, please!

BUD: Fuck? Fuck's bad? We don't say it, we just do it, huh? (DEXTER *comes in, now in Sunday clericals*)

DEXTER: Behold, the Bridegroom cometh!

SAM: Good morning, Dexter.

DEXTER: I'm here to conduct you to chapel.

SAM: You must think we need it.

DEXTER: Oh, I've walked in on worse in my thirty-odd years at the school.

BUD: I'll bet you have.

DEXTER (*to* SAM): I'm doing the sermon today. The Rector has awarded me that privilege.

SAM (*as he ties his tie*): You obviously run the joint, Dexter. You should be Rector yourself.

DEXTER: I put myself up for it, you know. During the last search. I proposed myself as an in-house candidate.

SAM: How'd you come out?

DEXTER: Fine, for a while. I was a finalist in the selection process. I had high hopes.

SAM: What happened? Why'd they pick that fatuous glad-hander over you?

DEXTER: Oh well. You see, he was married. I wasn't. It came down to that.

SAM: Ah. (*Pause*)

BUD (*who has been looking out*): I notice a TV van out there.

DEXTER: Oh yes. I meant to say.

BUD: You meant to say what?

DEXTER: Mrs. Pell wants some sense of the occasion.

BUD: I thought we agreed.

DEXTER: It's strictly local news. And the cameras will remain unobtrusively in the rear.

BUD: Which means they'll commandeer the front row. And go national if they can.

DEXTER: Oh now. Let's be more charitable with our brethren of the press.

SAM: Let's at least go to church. . . . You coming, Bud?

BUD: I already hit early Mass in town.

SAM: Go for the Double Feature.

BUD: No thanks.

SAM: Come on. It's a gorgeous service. The rich, compelling language of the Book of Common Prayer. . . . "We have left undone those things which we ought to have done. And we have done those things which we ought not to have done. And there is no health in us."

DEXTER: Good for you, Sam. Letter-perfect.

BUD: It's a great sound-bite, Sam. You could base your campaign on it.

SAM: Go back to bed, Bud.

BUD: I'm awake, man! You're the one who's asleep. (*He goes out*)

DEXTER: What an insistent young man.

SAM: He'll go far.

DEXTER: I envy the Catholics. They see things so clearly. Martin Luther made it all much more difficult when he put us in charge of our own salvation. (*More church bells*) Well. We should go.

SAM: Lead, kindly light. (*He goes into the bedroom for his jacket*)

DEXTER: You might be interested to know that I'm speaking today on Saint Paul.

SAM (*from bedroom*): Hey! My buddy!

DEXTER: Yes. I dug up the sermon I gave the year you graduated. I explore how Paul moves beyond the erotic to a larger kind of love.

SAM: Sounds like just my meat. (*They go off, as* HARRIET *comes on, followed by* PERRY. *She is dressed for graduation, He wears a senior blazer and slacks, and carries a sports trophy with a tennis player mounted on top*)

HARRIET: There he goes! Cut him loose from the herd!

PERRY (*calling out*): Sam! Hey, Sam! (SAM *comes on, now in his graduation blazer*) Mother wants to see you.

SAM (*hugging him; indicating the trophy*): Congratulations, man! The tennis trophy! What did I tell ya?

PERRY: Where's your Leadership Cup?

SAM: I left it with my father. He wants it for mixing martinis.

HARRIET: Hail to the chief who in triumph advances. (*She shakes* SAM's *hand*) I simply want to congratulate you, Sam, for walking off with every prize in the school.

PERRY: Except the tennis trophy, Mother.

HARRIET: Oh well, that was a foregone conclusion.

PERRY: I wish I'd won the Drama Cup.

HARRIET: I'm delighted you didn't, Darling. (*To* SAM) Now, Sam: what new worlds will you conquer next?

SAM: Princeton, I hope.

HARRIET: You hope? Aren't you sure?

SAM: My father's had some setbacks lately. We had to apply for a scholarship. If I don't get it, I'll end up at State.

HARRIET: Surely it's time to pull a few strings.

SAM: Those strings are getting a little frayed these days.

HARRIET: I wish you could join Perry at Middlebury.

PERRY: I wish I'd gotten into Columbia.

HARRIET: Nonsense. Middlebury is the perfect solution. They have skiing, they have square dancing . . .

SAM: They have girls.

HARRIET: Exactly, Sam. They are co-educational. Which means hundreds of lovely girls, all there waiting to be kissed . . .

PERRY: Maybe they're there for other reasons, Mother.

HARRIET: Maybe they are. . . . Now Perry, Dear, I wonder if you'd go stand in that line, and get us one of those delicious-looking fruit punches on this hot June day?

SAM: I'll do it.

HARRIET: No, I want Perry to do it. Would you, Dear? For your mother and your Old Boy?

PERRY (*saluting*): Aye, aye, sir. (*Goes off*)

HARRIET (*watching him go*): That, Sam, is your doing.

SAM: What?

HARRIET: That. The whole thing. The tennis prize, Middlebury, the confident way he walks. I put it all down to you, Sam. You've been a marvelous Old Boy.

SAM: That was just the first year, Mrs. Pell. Now he's one of my best friends.

HARRIET: There are friends and there are friends, Sam.

SAM: No, I'm serious. We would've roomed together this year, except I can't stand the *Forza Del Destino*.

HARRIET: It's that *Forza* thing we've still got to fight, Sam. All the way to the finish.

SAM: Excuse me?

HARRIET: Tell me. What are your plans for the summer, Sam?

SAM: Teaching sailing, actually.

HARRIET: Teaching *sailing!*

SAM: On the Vineyard.

HARRIET: On Martha's Vineyard! What fun.

SAM: I visited there last summer, and this summer I got the sailing job at the Yacht Club.

HARRIET: How enterprising, Sam.

SAM: It's a job, anyway. And I like it there.

HARRIET: Perry wants to spend his summer in New York.

SAM: So he said.

HARRIET: He says if he can't go to Columbia, he can still do that.

SAM: Sounds fair to me.

HARRIET: Taking some stupid course on Medieval music.

SAM: He loves music.

HARRIET: It does not seem like a terribly healthy summer to me, sitting around that hot, dirty city, listening to monks sing madrigals.

SAM: It's what he wants.

HARRIET: Of course, his father's there. Who now claims to be a photographer. And lives with an Italian woman half his age. And hardly gives Perry the time of day.

SAM: Perry likes him, though.

HARRIET: I know. (*Pause*) It's hard not to. (*Pause*) Sam, have you ever been out west?

SAM: No.

HARRIET: Would you like to go?

SAM: Of course.

HARRIET: All right now, Sam. Here's the thing. I would like it very much if you took Perry on a good, long trip out west this summer.

SAM: Oh I couldn't—

HARRIET: No, now wait. I will give you the Buick station wagon, and *carte blanche* financially. My Aunt Esther has a ranch in Montana and you can stop there for as long as you want. You can fish, you can ride, you can even work if you feel like it. Or you can move on. You can go to Nevada and gamble. You can go to Wyoming and visit the brothels. You can end up in

Hollywood, I don't care, just as long as you go. I think it will be good for you, I know it will be good for Perry.

SAM: Wow!

HARRIET: There you are.

SAM: Except I've already got this job.

HARRIET: I should imagine, Sam, that there are twenty other boys who would give their eyeteeth to teach sailing on Martha's Vineyard.

SAM: There's another thing, though.

HARRIET: What other thing?

SAM: I've got this girl, Mrs. Pell.

HARRIET: Ah. The Girl.

SAM: We're kind of going together.

HARRIET: Yes. Perry told me about The Girl.

SAM: She's the real reason I got the job down there.

HARRIET: Ah yes. Now let's see if I've got the facts straight. You met her there last summer, and her father owns a hardware store, and she came up to some dance.

SAM: Right.

HARRIET: Perry said he treated you both to dinner at the Inn. He said she was very attractive.

SAM: She thought Perry was terrific.

HARRIET: And I'm sure she thinks you're *more* than terrific.

SAM: We get along.

HARRIET: Well then she'll keep.

SAM: Keep?

HARRIET: While you go west.

SAM: Could I bring her along?

HARRIET: No, Sam. That might be a little tricky.

SAM: Then I don't know . . .

HARRIET: I'll tell you something else, Sam. There need be no more difficulty about Princeton. I know a man on the Board of Trustees, and I'll sing him your praises.

SAM: What if Perry doesn't want to go west?

HARRIET: He'll go, if you go. (*Pause.* SAM *thinks*)

SAM: This is a tough one, Mrs. Pell.

HARRIET: It's the tough ones that are worth winning, Sam.

SAM: O.K. I'll do it.

HARRIET: Would you, Sam? That is princely of you. Princely. Of a Princeton man. . . . Now I want to meet your parents. I want to tell them they've produced a prince among men.

SAM: Just my father's here. My stepmother couldn't make it.

HARRIET: Oh dear. Not ill, I hope.

SAM: Oh no. She's down south, marching for civil rights.

HARRIET: What fun. Well, then I'll tell your *father* he's produced a prince among men.

SAM: He won't agree.

HARRIET: What? Doesn't he appreciate you?

SAM: He thinks I could stand some improvement.

HARRIET (*taking his arm*): Oh well, all parents think that about their children. (*They go off, as* PERRY *comes out in khakis and a flannel shirt. He shouts for* SAM *a number of times, as if they were in great open space. Then he goes to the bench and honks the "horn" as if it were a car*)

PERRY (*calling off*): Come on! We haven't got all day! (*He honks again. Other car sounds are heard passing, as if he were parked along a highway. Finally* SAM *enters, now in a pullover shirt*) Where the hell have you been?

SAM: I was talking to those babes we met on the trail.

PERRY: I've been waiting for half an hour.

SAM: They want to party.

PERRY: Can't.

SAM: They have beer.

PERRY: Can't, Sam. Have to make Sacramento by four tomorrow.

SAM: They have beer, they have burgers.

PERRY: We've got to sell the car and make a four o'clock plane. Now get the hell IN.

SAM (*looking over his shoulder*): We could catch another plane. There are plenty of planes. You think there's just one plane?

PERRY: I've got to make Freshman week.

SAM: What's Freshman week? That's for high school guys. You're beyond that shit, Perry. You're a big boy now.

PERRY: In, Sam. Please. (SAM *reluctantly gets in the car;* PERRY *starts to turn the key.* SAM *grabs his hand*)

SAM: The dark-haired one thought you were cute, Perry.

PERRY: She did not.

SAM: She did. She said, "Where's your cute friend?"

PERRY: She didn't say that.

SAM: She said, "Where's your cute friend? I want to open my throbbing loins to him, tonight, under the Western stars."

PERRY (*starting the car; they jerk forward*): Bullshit. (*They drive*)

SAM: So where will we camp tonight then?

PERRY: On the way somewhere.

SAM: What'll we do? Toast marshmallows? Tell ghost stories?

PERRY: Jesus, Sam. There's such a thing as making conversation.

SAM (*looking back*): O.K. I'll begin. Seen any good-looking girls lately?

PERRY: Very funny. (*They drive*) I keep thinking about next year.

SAM: I keep thinking about back there.

PERRY: I'll bet we don't connect much next year. Different colleges, different friends. I'll bet we don't see each other much any more.

SAM (*mock sentimental*): "I'll be seeing you, in all the old familiar places . . ." (*He turns on the "radio." We hear classical music. He finds a ball game. At an exciting moment,* PERRY *turns it off*) Hey! Come on!

PERRY: You really piss me off sometimes, Sam. You know that?

SAM: Yeah well don't get so corny, then.

PERRY: Just because I have feelings, I'm corny. Just because I value our friendship, I'm now corny.

SAM: Change the channel, Perry.

PERRY: Sometimes I think you're a cold son of a bitch, Sam. You really are a cold, thoughtless guy sometimes.

SAM: Oooh. Ouch. What brought that on?

PERRY: You leave me standing there while you shoot the breeze with a couple of babes. You always have to listen to the fucking Red Socks, but when an opera comes on, we have to turn it right off . . .

SAM: Oh for Chrissake.

PERRY: And when we were at the ranch, you kept going after that waitress . . .

SAM: What's wrong with that?

PERRY: You didn't even *like* her. You *said* you didn't like her. And yet you screwed her, you son of a bitch.

SAM: So what if I did?

PERRY: You never even told her goodbye.

SAM: That was an oversight.

PERRY: That was shitty, Sam. That was shitty behavior.

SAM: Just because you . . .

PERRY: Because I what?

SAM: Don't care about girls.

PERRY: I care about girls. I cared about that girl. I cared about her more than you did.

SAM: Then why don't you care about those girls back THERE? Why, during this whole trip, whenever there's a chance to go out with girls, you're always backing off, for Chrissake?

PERRY: Bullshit, Sam. Apply the bullshit quotient, please.

SAM: You're always backing off. I mean, when we were in Reno, and had that chance to go to that cat house, you wanted to go to *Lawrence of Arabia!* I mean, what are you? A fag, or what? (PERRY *jams on the brakes; Both lurch forward*)

PERRY: I'm not a fag, Sam.

SAM: Those girls are just SITTING there, waiting for us to make our MOVE!

PERRY: I'm not a fag.

SAM: Well I mean, you've got your problems, Perry.

PERRY (*hitting him on the arm*): I'm not a fag.

SAM (*hitting him back*): Hey! Knock it off!

PERRY: Get out of the car!

SAM: Says who?

PERRY: Me! Get out of my goddam car, Sam!

SAM (*getting out*): O.K. Fine. I'll go back and see those girls! (*Through the "window"*) So long, fag.

PERRY (*jumping out of the car*): Don't call me that.

SAM (*going off*): Fag! Fag! Fairy Perry!

PERRY (*leaping on him*): Go fuck yourself, Sam! Go fuck yourself! (*They fight.* SAM *is stronger. He ultimately gets on top*)

SAM: Or should I fuck YOU, Perry? Want your Old Boy to fuck you? Huh? Huh? (*He plants a big kiss on* PERRY's *lips*) How's that? Is that what you want? (PERRY *rolls free. They both get up, separate. Sounds of traffic going by are heard periodically*)

PERRY: I'm not a fag, Sam!

SAM: O.K., O.K. I'm sorry.

PERRY: I don't know what I am. But I'm not that.

SAM: O.K., O.K. (*Pause*) I think the trouble with us, the trouble with both of us, is we just need more sex. Men don't get sex, they get frustrated and fight among themselves. It happens with rats. (*Pause*) Now here we are out west the summer before we go to college, and you're constantly bringing me down as far as girls are concerned, and so naturally, I just blew up.

PERRY: Just leave it, Sam. O.K.

SAM: I mean, that's why I thought you should see those babes. Our last chance out here, and I thought you should have a sexual experience. That's all I thought, and I'll bet your mother would agree with me.

PERRY: I've had a sexual experience.

SAM: Yeah, yeah.

PERRY: O.K. Don't believe me then.

SAM: When?

PERRY: That's my business.

SAM: Not this summer, that's for sure.

PERRY: Last summer, if you must know. While you were having yours.

SAM: When you went to New York?

PERRY: Right.

SAM: Do I know her?

PERRY: No.

SAM: Did you get in?

PERRY: No.

SAM: But you came close?

PERRY: Maybe.

SAM: Where'd you meet her?

PERRY: At a friend's.

SAM: What friend?

PERRY: We met at my father's.

SAM: She was a friend of your father's?

PERRY: Right.

SAM: Oh my God! An older woman! Did she show you the ropes? Remember *Room at the Top*?

PERRY: Yes.

SAM: Jesus. Sneaky Pete here. Last summer he's learning the ropes from Simone Signoret! How come you didn't tell me?

PERRY: I don't have to tell you everything.

SAM: Thought I'd tease you about it?

PERRY: Maybe.

SAM: You like her, don't you? That's why you turned down those babes. You like her. I can tell.

PERRY: It's not a her, Sam.

SAM: Not a her?

PERRY: I was sleeping on the couch over at my father's, and this friend of his got in bed with me.

SAM: Jesus! Did you kick him out?

PERRY: Sure. Oh sure. That's what I did. Immediately.

SAM: You told your dad, I hope.

PERRY: No.

SAM: My dad would've gone through the ROOF!

PERRY: My dad's kind of loose about things, actually.

SAM: But God! It must've been GROSS! Did he touch your dong?

PERRY: No. Of course not. No.

SAM: So. Ho hum. Big deal. What are you? Scarred for life? That make you scarred for life?

PERRY: No.

SAM: O.K. Then it's water over the dam.

PERRY: It's not over the dam yet.

SAM: What? He's still bothering you?

PERRY: Not bothering me.

SAM: Whatever you call it, there are laws against it, Perry.

PERRY: Are there laws against going to plays?

SAM: What are you talking about?

PERRY: Remember when I got special permission from school to see the Royal Shakespeare? This guy got the tickets.

SAM: Jesus. And you went!

PERRY: I wanted to see the play.

SAM: You are grossing me out here, Perry. You are definitely grossing me out. Did you have a sexual encounter?

PERRY: I don't want to talk about it.

SAM: You did, didn't you? You had a sexual encounter with this guy.

PERRY: All right. I did.

SAM: Oh my God! This is total gross-out time!

PERRY: Well you might as well know I'm meeting him in New York tomorrow night!

SAM: Is that why you wanted to get back?

PERRY: Yes!

SAM: Oh my God.

PERRY: I like him, Sam. I like him more than you ever liked that waitress at the ranch.

SAM: I can't believe I'm hearing this.

PERRY: Yeah, well, he wants me to come down from Middlebury and see him this fall, and stay at his place and go to the opera with him, too, if I want to!

SAM: And you want to?

PERRY: I don't know what I want.

SAM: Get in the car. Get in the CAR, Perry! My turn to drive. (*They get back in the car;* SAM *drives*) You were right, what you said back there, Perry. About maybe not seeing each other much after this. . . . Because I have to tell you, Perry, if you start hanging out with guys like that, and going to the opera all the time, if that's what you want, then count me out.

PERRY: I'm not sure I want that.

THE OLD BOY

SAM: Well, I know what I want. I want to walk into a room with a pretty girl on my arm, and know that she's mine for the evening. I want to get married some day, and have great sex three times a night, and even during the day. I want to have kids, and dogs, and play sports on weekends, and be a respected leader in my community. I want to move on up and contribute something positive to my country and the world. Maybe you think that's bullshit, but that's what I want.

PERRY: I want that, too. You think I don't want that? I want that every minute of the day. I see a guy getting cozy with a girl, I envy him. I see a baby carriage, I think that's never for me. I see a house, just some dumb *house* for shit's sake, and I wonder if I'll ever live in one, and who would ever live there with me.

SAM: Oh come on.

PERRY: It's true, Sam. . . . And at night, I have these feelings . . . these other feelings . . . these strong feelings . . . about guys . . . sometimes even about you, Sam . . .

SAM: Me? Jesus, Perry. . . . What—do you have us doing?

PERRY: We—make love.

SAM: Am I any good?

PERRY: I'm serious, Sam!

SAM: I know. Go on.

PERRY: I have these feelings. And I pray, I PRAY—I don't believe in any of that horseshit—but I pray to God that He will take . . . that He will BURN these feelings out of me forever and ever, and send me some GIRL, and we'll fall in love, and live happily ever after.

SAM: I know a girl who likes you a lot.

PERRY: Yeah? Who?

SAM: Alison.

PERRY: Alison?

SAM: She likes you a lot. (*Pause*) Do you like her?

PERRY: Of course.

SAM: You sure said you did when I brought her up to school.

PERRY: I like her a lot.

SAM: Take her out if you want.

PERRY: Take Alison out?

SAM: You'd be a great pair.

PERRY: I thought you liked her.

SAM: My father wants me to cool it.

PERRY: But she likes *you.*

THE OLD BOY

SAM: She thinks you're a fascinating guy.

PERRY: She thinks I'm a big spender.

SAM: "A fascinating guy." Those were her exact words.

PERRY: She said that?

SAM: I swear. Now think positively. Take your sexual desires and refocus them on Alison.

PERRY: I thought she was your girl.

SAM: I'm not ready for a steady relationship.

PERRY: That's for sure.

SAM: Actually, you'd be getting me off the hook.

PERRY: We got along, didn't we? Alison and me. That time.

SAM: I couldn't get a word in edgewise.

PERRY: I told her we were kindred spirits.

SAM: There you are. Kindred spirits. Hey, suppose I fix you up with her. I'm seeing her in New York next week. I'll work something out. Meanwhile, you tell your faggy friend to bug off . . .

PERRY: I'll say I've got a previous engagement.

SAM: O.K. Say that. And hey! Alison's going to the University of Vermont this fall. You could drive over from Middlebury in that new Corvette your mother promised you. She loves Corvettes. She told me. You'll snow the pants off her. So see? It's perfect! Your prayers are answered, Buddy!

PERRY: Right.

SAM: So. We are no longer doooomed to hang around bars with creeps in New York, and listen to the Farts of Destiny. We're rejoining the human race. Is it a deal?

PERRY: It's a deal, Sam. It's a real deal.

SAM (pulling over): Fine. Now let's pull over and take a good manly pee. Those beers with those babes have caught up with me. (SAM stops the car. The exit. Traffic sounds are heard, then drowned out by: A hymn: "For the Beauty of the Earth . . ." ALISON comes on, holding a cup of coffee; she looks around. The hymn fades as HARRIET enters)

HARRIET: What are you doing out here?

ALISON: Getting a little fresh air.

HARRIET: Alison, dear, I'm not sure it's a good idea to be stalking around, in front of all these students, with a cup of coffee in your hand. You look a little . . . disconnected. Come back into the vestry.

ALISON: No thanks.

HARRIET: Then I wonder if you might tell me what in heaven's name is the matter. You've contradicted me all weekend. I thought we were a solid front, you and I. Do you think our dear Perry would be happy if he knew his mother and his wife had suddenly started bickering in public?

ALISON: I'm not sure.

HARRIET: Well, *I'm* sure of several things, Alison. I'm sure that life will be much pleasanter for both of us if we don't argue. I'm sure that those handsome checks which land on your doorstep every Christmas are not based on your being disagreeable. I'm sure that my grandson's future is at least somewhat dependent on you and I pulling together. (*She sees* SAM, *who enters, now dressed in his suit*) Ah, dear Sam! Come inside before the graduation march. We're having coffee and rolls.

ALISON: The coffee's weak, the rolls are repulsive.

HARRIET: Alison—I think you and I should probably continue our own conversation on the trip back down to the real world. (*She takes* ALISON's *cup and goes*)

ALISON (*to* SAM): I've been waiting to waylay you.

SAM: Uh-oh. Do you plan to keep your shoes on?

ALISON: I'll try. . . . Are you all right, by the way?

SAM: I think so.

ALISON: I was watching you all during chapel. You just sat and stared. And then disappeared.

SAM: I took a walk around the pond.

ALISON: Thinking about your speech?

SAM: Thinking about lots of things. I was a manipulative bastard, wasn't I?

ALISON: Oh hell, I made my own bed, too. Though I didn't get much sleep in it last night.

SAM: I wish I could make things up to you.

ALISON: You can, actually. That's why I'm waylaying you. I wonder if you could get me a job.

SAM: A job?

ALISON: Through your Old Boy network. I can't live this way any longer. I want to earn my own keep. Which means a job. I suppose I could slink back to the Clamshell, but I like to think I've grown beyond it.

SAM: Let's see. . . . Who do I know in the shoe business?

ALISON: No, I'm serious. I can't type, or work a computer, or do any of those things. But I'm smart. And still ambitious.

SAM: I'll check around.

ALISON: I'd be wonderful in the State Department. After all, I've maintained a diplomatic front for over half my life.

SAM: Until last night.

ALISON: Lookit, I've been in analysis long enough to know that you don't get that mad at people unless you feel pretty strongly about them.

SAM: I'll buy that.

ALISON: So. Suppose we work it this way. You find me a job, any job, anywhere, and we'll forgive and forget. Or rather remember—the good things. There's something between us, Sam. There was on the Vineyard, and there was in your room last night. We might even see each other occasionally . . . (*Pause*) I mean, if I worked in Washington . . . (*Pause*) Or even if I didn't. (*Pause*) Oh Lord. Now I feel I'm back at the Whaler Bar, pleading for your attention.

SAM: I'll try to find you a job, Alison.

ALISON: Thank you.

SAM: But I can't see you again.

ALISON: Why not?

SAM: Perry.

ALISON: Perry's dead now.

A. R. *Gurney*

SAM: So am I. (HARRIET, DEXTER *and* BUD *join them.* DEXTER *wears an academic robe, and carries another, along with a purple hood. They all talk almost at once*)

DEXTER: All rightee! Time to gird up our loins! (*He begins to drape* SAM *with an academic robe*)

BUD (*to* SAM): What did I tell you? That TV crowd has moved right in.

HARRIET: Sam, dear, when you mention the tennis court, say I'm thinking of a clay surface. It gives a truer bounce. Be sure you mention clay.

DEXTER (*fussing with the robes*): Hath not the potter power over the clay? Paul. Romans. Nine, Twenty-one.

ALISON (*low to* SAM): Are you sure you're all right?

DEXTER (*adjusting a purple hood*): We couldn't decide which of your honorary degrees to reflect in your hood. The purple from Williams, or the blue from Yale.

BUD (*handing* SAM *a stack of note cards*): You can fall back on these if you get into trouble.

DEXTER (*adjusting the hood*): We finally chose Williams. The imperial purple seemed particularly appropriate.

SAM: Dexter, did Paul say the truth shall set thee free?

DEXTER (*as he fusses with the robes*): No, that was Christ. In the Fourth Gospel. Why?

SAM: I can't get it out of my head. (*A trumpet fanfare is heard*)

DEXTER: Ah, the trumpet soundeth. . . . Mrs. Pell, if you would stand over there, behind the Class Marshall . . .

HARRIET: Absolutely. (HARRIET *goes off*)

DEXTER: And Mrs. Pell, Junior, if you would stand beside her . . .

ALISON: All right. (ALISON *goes off.* DEXTER *turns to* BUD)

DEXTER: And you, sir, have a reserved seat out in front.

BUD: Right. I see it. Out by the parking lot. (BUD *goes off the opposite side. The lights focus in on* SAM *and* DEXTER)

DEXTER: And now Sam, what will happen is that we'll march over to the dais, and then we'll have the prayers, and the hymn, and the handing out of diplomas, and then the awarding of the prizes, and then the Rector will make the introduction, and you'll speak. It's as simple as that. (DEXTER *is out by now.* SAM *is alone on stage, as if on the speaker's platform*)

SAM: Thank you, Doctor Fayerweather . . . . (*Carefully*) Members of the faculty . . . members of the graduating class . . . students . . . parents . . . distinguished guests . . . babies . . . golden retrievers . . . and squirrels. (*Pause. He glances at* BUD'*s notes, then rejects them, tucking them away in his jacket*) When I was a boy here, we were always looking for the right answers. Sometimes they were in the back of the algebra book. "If A works twice as hard as B," and so forth, and the answer would always be some neat, round number, like 4, and it was our job to show how we arrived at it. And at the end of the school year, we'd take exams, and neatly circle all our answers, fold our blue books and sign the pledge on the outside: "I pledge my honor, as a gentleman, that I have neither given nor received help." (*Pause*) We also found answers at home, when we returned for vacation. "If I go out on a date, what time do I have to be home?" The answer was twelve. "What's wrong with Communism?" It's evil. "What must I do to earn your love and respect?" Work twice as hard as B. Always there were answers. And if neither the school nor our family could provide them, we still assumed they were there, somewhere on down the line, at Harvard, in Washington, or in Heaven. (*Pause*) Today we're lucky if we find the right questions. Maybe that's all a good school can do these days—teach us good questions. At least, since I've been back, it's taught me to ask a few. And maybe now it's time for me to take an exam on them. After all, as Mr. MacDonald over there used to say in Classy Civ, "The unexamined life is not worth living." O.K.? So here's my final exam. (*Pause*) First question. Big question. Huge subject. Love in the Western World. What in God's name is our problem? Why do we worry so much about unconventional forms of love? Are we afraid of love? Are we threatened by it when it stands out from the crowd? Here at school, we studied those long, bloody wars fought over religion. This country was founded as a haven from these wars. If we so cherish religious tolerance, why not sexual tolerance as well? Will there be a time when people's sexual natures are considered matters for their own soul, like their religion? Answer: let's hope. (*Pause*) Next question. What about the AIDS epidemic? Is this the result of sexual freedom, or sexual repression? By maligning gay people, any group of people, have we caused them to turn in on themselves in self-destructive ways? And by doing this, by creating these ghettoes, have we ghettoized ourselves, cutting ourselves off from the rich diversity which constitutes American life? I can see Mr. Burnham writing in the margin: "Interesting, if true." (*Pause*) Main question. Is there something in my own life which relates to all this? Yes. Oh yes. I can answer this one. When I was a boy here, I had a friend—a good friend— a gay friend—whom I persuaded to conform to a conventional life. Why? Was it natural? No. It was unnatural, to him. Was it right? No. It was wrong for him. Why did I do it, then? Was it something in me—some attempt to deny some passion in my own soul? Mr. Montgomery might add this comment: "Try to avoid cliches." (*Pause*) Final question. What happened to this boy? He died. Why did he die? From a desperate attempt to make up for lost time. Who is responsible for that? Me. I am responsible. I was his Old Boy. I had a special obligation. (*Pause*) "Bullshit," Perry might say. "Apply the bullshit quotient immediately." But I don't think I'm bullshitting now . . . (*Pause*) Optional question. Extra credit. What can I do about this? Nothing. Can I bring him back? No. Can I apologize to him? No. Too late, too late, too late. What then? . . . Oh Perry, why do I discover this now, only now, when there's nothing to do, nothing to be done . . . when I can never tell you . . . never say . . . never even . . . (*Stops, looks around*) I pledge my honor as a gentleman that I have neither given nor received. . . . Oh God. (*He covers his face with his hands. Then* DEXTER *appears solicitously, speaks to the audience*)

DEXTER: Perhaps we might conclude the ceremonies with another hymn. (*Calling off*) Would you start us off, Mr. Benbow? (*Starts singing, leading*) "Faith of our fathers, Holy Faith . . ." (*He puts an arm around* SAM *and helps him from the stage as the music and singing come up.* BUD *enters, dials the telephone*)

BUD: Hi. Looks like I'll be home for dinner. . . . Oh sure. We'll be out of here fast. . . . Because he booted the ball, Baby. I'll tell you when I get there . . . (*Knocking is heard off*) Someone's at the door. . . . We'll talk when I get home. . . . Hey. Keep the kids up, will you? Haven't seen them in centuries. . . . Love you, too . . . (*Hangs up; calls out*) Yo! It's open. (HARRIET *comes in*)

HARRIET: I'd like to speak to your lord and master.

BUD: He's taking a shower.

HARRIET: Well, I'm leaving. I wonder if you'd give him a message.

BUD: Shoot.

HARRIET: Tell him, if you would, that I have fought all my life against what is soft and sick and self-indulgent.

BUD: O.K.

HARRIET: Tell him that I left my husband, and raised my son, and hope to raise my grandson in the belief that there are such things as traditional values, decent behavior and basic self-control.

BUD: O.K.

HARRIET (*starts out, then turns*): You might also tell him that he's broken my heart. (*She goes, as we hear the sound of a shower and* SAM *singing*)

SAM'S VOICE: "Fling out the banner! Let it ride, Skyward and seaward, high and wide!"

(DEXTER *comes out from within*)

BUD: How's he doing?

DEXTER: Him that hath ears, let him hear. . . . . Perhaps you'd like to stay while I investigate the extent of the damage.

BUD: Sure. (DEXTER *goes off.* SAM *comes out in a terry cloth robe, towelling his hair. He crosses to get the Bible by the telephone*)

SAM: Where've you been?

BUD: Right here. Calling Katie.

SAM: Told her you'll take the new job, right?

BUD: Not yet.

SAM: Ah. (*Crossing back, he flashes at* BUD, *and exits*)

BUD: You O.K.?

SAM (*reentering*): Never better. It's weird. (*Exits again*)

BUD: Feel like talking shop?

SAM (*now off*): Sure. While I get dressed.

BUD (*speaking towards off*): O.K., here goes. I'm not worried about the local news. That won't matter much. Tomorrow, when it goes nationwide, that's when the trouble starts . . . "Well-bred"—Or will they say "White-bread—gubernatorial candidate delivers bizarre, highly emotional diatribe on gay rights at posh New England prep school." Not to mention the visual thing. (SAM *comes out in khakis and an informal shirt, carrying a Val-Pac and a windbreaker*)

SAM: The visual thing?

BUD: That moment at the end when you pulled your Muskie . . .

SAM: I never touched my muskie.

BUD: *Senator* Muskie, Sam. New Hampshire, '72. He cried. It cost him the primary. They called it "womanish behavior."

SAM (*putting on his shoes*): Maybe it got me the women's vote.

BUD: It got you the gay vote, Sam. If that. . . . The President will be very kind, of course. He'll give you a sad smile, and ask you to transfer to the Department of Health and Human Services.

SAM: I'll quit before he gets around to it.

BUD: O.K. So I'll call party headquarters, and say you're withdrawing. For personal reasons.

SAM: Withdrawing?

BUD: You don't still plan to go for it?

SAM: Sure. What's the problem?

BUD: Here's the problem, Sam. The media will say . . . carefully, of course, to avoid a libel suit . . . that you're gay as a goose.

SAM: They said that about Saint Paul.

BUD: Christ, Sam.

SAM: And about him, too.

BUD: Watch it, Pal.

SAM: You wait, Bud. They'll say it about you.

BUD: Fuck you, Sam.

SAM: Fuck you, Bud. (DEXTER *comes in*)

DEXTER: I keep walking in on the same scintillating exchange.

SAM: I've just discovered the pleasure of saying four-letter words.

DEXTER: It's a limited pleasure, and soon will pale. I've come to say a more significant word. Namely, goodbye.

SAM (*shaking hands*): So long, Dexter. I hope my speech didn't thoroughly disappoint you.

DEXTER: Well, I have to say that Mrs. Pell is giving her tennis court to Andover. And the Rector is thinking of removing your name from the list of distinguished alumni.

SAM: Yippee! That makes it official! I'm no longer an Old Boy!

DEXTER: As for me . . . if you want my opinion . . . (*Pause*) I was very moved by what you said. (*Pause*) It made me wonder if once upon a time, I should have . . . (*Pause*) But no. This is a good school, and I hope I've helped make it a better one.

SAM (*embracing him*): You have, Dexter. You have indeed. (ALISON *enters*)

ALISON: Well, what d'ya know?

SAM: What?

ALISON: What. The man says what. (*To* DEXTER *and* BUD) Here is a man I thought was buttoned up for life. I told him so, last night, right here in this room. And now, today, he's suddenly turning himself inside out and upside down in front of all America. (*To* SAM) That's what. You were great, sir.

SAM: You might have a slight disagreement about that with your mother-in-law.

ALISON: Already did. She wanted me to deny everything you said, or she'd cut me off without a cent.

SAM: What did you say?

ALISON: Never mind, but she left without me.

SAM: Then you need a ride.

ALISON: I've already found one. I ran into some folks who have room in their back seat of their green Volvo station wagon. They're headed in the general direction of my son's school. I'll stop there. Or rather start there . . . (*She starts out*)

SAM: Alison. I don't know how much clout I'll have now, but I owe you a job.

ALISON: I'll remember that. I'll also remember your speech for a long, long time. Thank you. (*She goes;* DEXTER *gets himself a glass of wine*)

SAM: Well, come on, Bud. Let's go.

BUD: What makes you think I'm going with you, Sam?

SAM: Because you love me. You admitted it yesterday.

BUD: I also admitted yesterday I work for winners. I see a loser here.

SAM: You need a ride back down, man.

BUD: I imagine, knowing this school, there's a chartered bus headed straight for Grand Central.

DEXTER: I'm afraid there is.

SAM: That's dumb, Bud.

BUD: Ten minutes in a car with you, you'd con me out of that new job and back onto your staff.

SAM: I'd sure try. (*A hymn is heard softly: "I Heard the Sound of Voices."*) Well, I'm off, then. (*Hugs* BUD) I'll miss you, Buddy. (*He starts out*)

BUD: Sam! You could at least tell me what your plans are.

SAM: I thought I'd stick my thumb up my ass and go on faith.

BUD: That's a compelling agenda for the '90s, Sam.

DEXTER: And a rather lonely notion, besides.

SAM: I got it from Paul. (*He goes*)

DEXTER (*to* BUD): That's not Paul. And he shouldn't say that it is.

BUD: He was kidding. (*Looks after* SAM) I think. (*He goes.* DEXTER *salutes them with his wine, as the music comes up and the lights dim*)

THE END